To Dad and Olivia – for the
hours spent searching for frogs.
And Diederik – for turning our
garden into a frog haven.

– S.F

For Devin, Steven and Roma.

– B.A

Also in the series:

First edition published in 2025 Flying Eye Books Ltd.
27 Westgate Street, London, E8 3RL.
www.flyingeyebooks.com

Represented by: Authorised Rep Compliance Ltd. Ground Floor,
71 Lower Baggot Street, Dublin, D02 P593, Ireland.
www.arccompliance.com

Text © Sara Forster 2025
Illustrations © Bianca Austria 2025

Sara Forster has asserted her right under the Copyright, Designs and Patents Act,
1988, to be identified as the Author of this Work. Bianca Austria has asserted her right under the
Copyright, Designs and Patents Act, 1988, to be identified as the Illustrator of this Work.

All rights reserved. No part of this publication may be reproduced or transmitted in any form
or by any means, electronic or mechanical, including photocopying, recording or by any
information and storage retrieval system, without prior written consent from the publisher.

Edited by Christina Webb
Designed by Tess Duffin

1 3 5 7 9 10 8 6 4 2

With special thanks to the Amphibian and Reptile Conservation Trust

Published in the US by Flying Eye Books Ltd.
Printed in China on FSC® certified paper.

UK ISBN: 978-1-83874-197-6

Sara Forster   Bianca Austria

Watch Me Grow

Frogs

Flying Eye Books

but what is a frog?

A frog is an **amphibian.** An amphibian is a **vertebrate,** which is an animal that has a backbone. Amphibians like frogs spend part of their lives in water and part on land.

Frogs, toads, newts and salamanders are all types of amphibians.

There are more than 6,000 different kinds of frogs.

Some frogs live in rainforests. These are called **tree frogs**.

Their bright, colourful skin tells **predators** to **"Watch out! I'm poisonous."**

Other frogs, like **common frogs**, live in wet places, near lakes and ponds. Their green and brown skin helps them to hide from hungry animals.

Can you spot the hiding frog?

But no matter where they live, they all have the same...

anatomy! A frog has...

Two big **eyes**.

Two **ear drums**.

A long, sticky **tongue**.

Ribbit! Ribbit!

A **vocal sac**.
Male frogs have a pouch that helps them make sounds. They fill it with air, just like you blow up a balloon.

croak!

Two short front **legs**.

Swimming

Jumping

Two strong back legs. In the water, a frog uses its back legs for swimming, and on land they help it to leap!

Smooth, damp **skin**.

Webbed feet. Frogs have large flaps of skin between the toes on their back feet to help them paddle.

But where is this little frog off to?

She's heading to the pond!

All frogs need fresh water to survive. Fresh water means that there is no salt in the water like there is in the sea. Freshwater **habitats** can be rivers, streams, lakes and ponds. These are also home to fish, mammals, birds and insects.

The floating leaves of a waterlily are called **lily pads**. Lily pads are good resting spots for frogs.

Dragonflies eat insects found around the pond.

Logs and stones make good hiding places for small fish like **minnows**.

Ducks also have webbed feet to help them paddle easily through the water.

A **kingfisher** uses a perch such as a branch to look for fish to catch.

SPLASH

With a SPLASH she leaps into the pond...

and starts swimming!

With their strong back legs and big, webbed feet, frogs are excellent swimmers. In fact, they are such good swimmers that humans copy the way a frog moves when we swim breaststroke.

First, they bring their back legs up towards their bodies...

then they drive their legs backwards, pushing against the water with their webbed feet while reaching forward with their front legs.

Then they bend their knees again, pulling their legs in, and tuck their front legs against their body, ready to start again.

This little frog is looking for somewhere special, somewhere...

to lay her eggs!

In the spring, frogs lay hundreds or even thousands of tiny black eggs.

She lays her eggs in the shallow water around the edge of the pond, hidden among plants like pondweed and reeds. This helps to keep the eggs safe.

These little eggs don't have shells. Instead, they are covered in a clear jelly. The eggs and jelly are called **frogspawn**.

The jelly helps to keep the eggs safe and warm, and stops them from drying out as they float on the surface of the water.

But look very closely and you'll start to see...

that the little black eggs are changing shape!

After two to four weeks the eggs have turned from small dots into tiny tadpoles.

They wiggle their way out of the jelly into the pond.

Each tadpole now has a long tail for swimming, and tiny whiskers called **gills** that help them to breathe underwater.

Unlike frogs, the tadpoles must find their food in the water.

First, they eat the jelly from around the eggs.

Then they eat any bits of plants and algae they find in the water. They are going to need lots of food to turn into a frog.

As the tadpoles start to grow...

their bodies begin to change shape.

First, they grow bigger... and bigger.

Then, after six to eight weeks they start to grow back legs.

Next, two front legs start to appear.

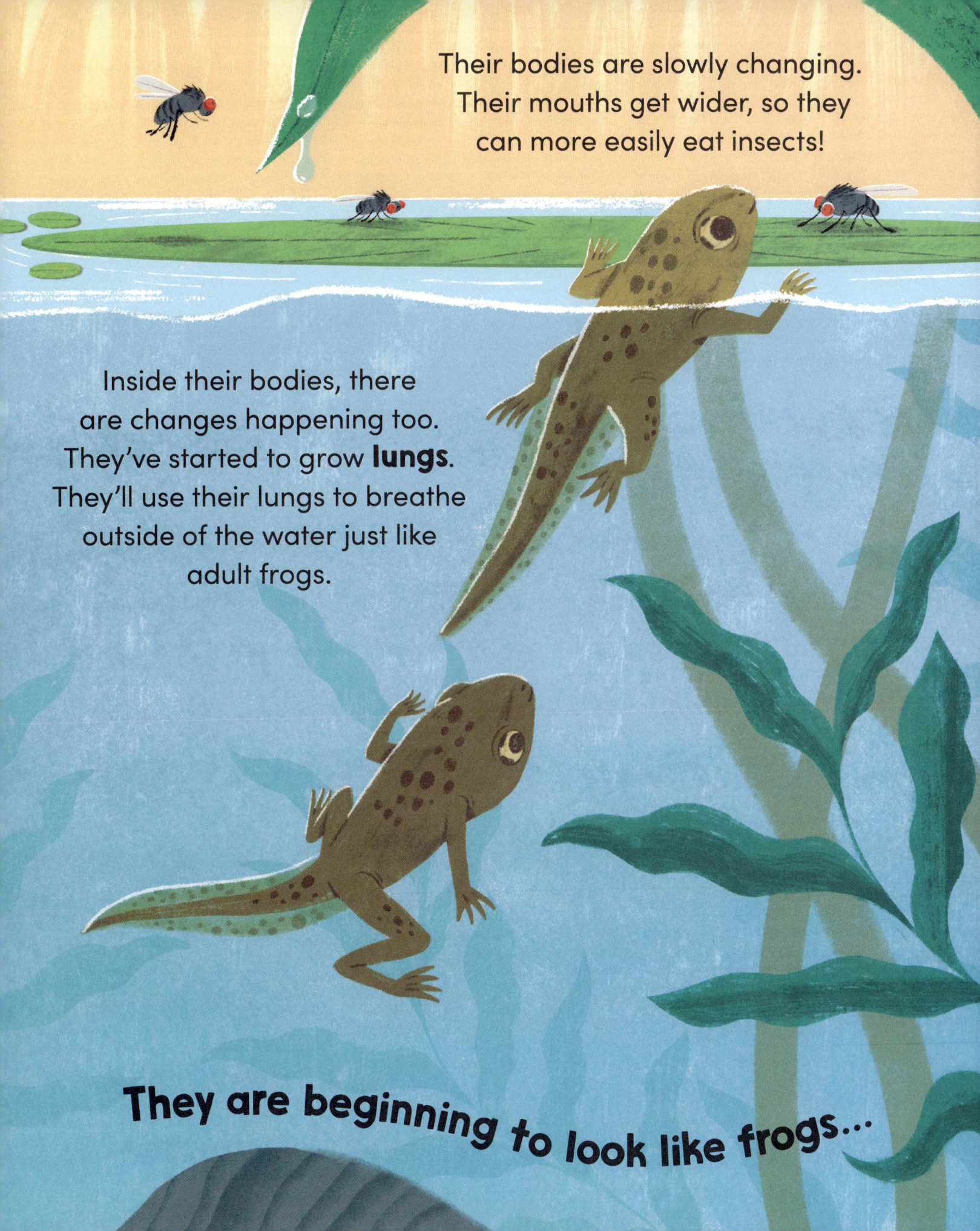

Their bodies are slowly changing. Their mouths get wider, so they can more easily eat insects!

Inside their bodies, there are changes happening too. They've started to grow **lungs**. They'll use their lungs to breathe outside of the water just like adult frogs.

They are beginning to look like frogs...

At around 14 weeks old, the froglet is now ready for life on land.

The little froglet leaps out of the water...

and finds something to eat!

Frogs have a special way of catching food.

When a frog spots what it wants to eat, it uses its strong back legs to leap towards its food...

Small frogs eat insects like flies and moths as well as snails, slugs and worms.

Glossary

Amphibian
An animal that can live on land and in water.

Frogspawn
The eggs of a frog, which are surrounded by transparent jelly.

Gills
The part of a fish or tadpole's body that it breathes through.

Habitat
An animal or a plant's habitat is the place where it naturally lives or grows.

Lungs
The part of your body (or an animal's body) used for breathing.

Predator
An animal that hunts other animals.

Vertebrate
An animal with a backbone.